AERODYNAMICS

poems by

Gail Ghai

Finishing Line Press
Georgetown, Kentucky

AERODYNAMICS

For Ravi
Who always carries a light
even in his shadow

ACKNOWLEDGMENTS

I am indebted to the editors of the following journals in which these poems first appeared:

Adana: "Designs"
Afterthought: "Daughter Cell"
Ariel: "Wedding Photo, 1941"
Burningwood Journal: "The First Boy I Kissed"
Dalhousie Review: "Two Phone Calls"
Descant: "Bagels," "That Cobalt Button"
Heron Clan XI: "Poetic Dust."
Icarus: "The Blue Dials," "Dark Wings"
Intense Experience: Social Psychology through Poetry, Oyster Press: "Jasper National Park"
Loyalhanna Review: 'Sunderance"
Minerva Rising: "Her Sunflower Apron"
Mother Jones: "What We Do for Our Children"
Pittsburgh Post Gazette: "Runway Lights"
Poetworks: Essential Love; Grayson Books: "The Last Star"
Sisyphus: "Elements"
Squaw Valley Review: "Dear Miss Manners"
Stone:stone: "Zigzag"
Taproot: "Johnny Two Feathers"
Tempus: "Summer Pie"
Writing in a Woman's Voice: "Ace of Diamonds"

Publisher: Leah Huete de Maines
Editor: Christen Kincaid
Cover Art: iStockPhoto.com
Author Photo: Ravi K Ghai
Cover Design: Elizabeth Maines McCleavy

Order online: www.finishinglinepress.com
also available on amazon.com

Author inquiries and mail orders:
Finishing Line Press
PO Box 1626
Georgetown, Kentucky 40324
USA

Contents

WEDDING PHOTO, 1941

Garbed in his handsome RCAF uniform,
gold shoulder wings angled for flight,
my father wears a triumphant grin.

His head is thrown back
in full flood light.
My mother wears a war-blue

gabardine suit.
Ivory laces the collar.
Swords of gladiolus guard her breasts.

Beneath a netted hat
she pauses on the edge
of a dazzling smile.

I blink, the photo blurs…I watch
her slow white pumps
to the altar.

Her left hand quivering
as she removes her pale glove.
Light trembles above her face

then shatters
into squares of a stained
glass window.

Behind her,
the palms of Christ
are blinded with blue light.

Her eyes moisten with panic.
It is the moment
of her swept-back veil.

AERODYNAMICS

When I was three and a half,
and had been flying
for over an hour

in my father's silver
and red Cessna, I asked:
When will we leave the ground?

My father roared.
My mother cackled.
My older brother chuckled.

Sitting small in the back seat
what did I know of aerodynamics?
Uplift, thrust, or drag?

I only knew the weight
of adult friction.
Their soaring tall bodies,

pitch of their constant voices
that cracked
the night air.

Rotation of silence
that always
followed.

My mother,
the left wing.
My father, the right,

but never quite
stabilizing
to give me lift.

THAT COBALT BUTTON

Up, the Down escalator
my sisters and I bounded
ignoring the irritated clicks
and clucks
of white gloved women
as we readied to alight
into the shoe department
of *Woodward's*.

Barbara, the boss, went first.
She pressed that cobalt button
and in a white flash
saw the red radiating lines
of her foot bones.
Saw what we all saw,
our skeletal futures.

Over and over, she flashed
the corpuscular light,
that crimson energy of atoms.
What did we know
of magnetic motion? A cloud chamber?
Nuclear track plates?
We didn't even know how to **spell** ionization
or heating effect, tissue
damage.

So, we took turns
pressing and pressing,
charging
and beaming.
And I took the most.

JASPER NATIONAL PARK

Our faces follow our father's commanding finger.
Mother's strapped with Kodak, recording his orders.
Our heads downward, watching as he launched

a spinning mini-boulder.
It rolled with a thunder's under roar
spinning gravel and dust, spinning

fear as it shattered
stone upon stone
to a plunging death below.

"How'd ya like to be that rock?" My father demanded.
His eyebrows arching as his grin widened
like a clown's painted smirk.

Always a dare. Always a hazard.
On the same trip he fed marshmallows
to drooling black bear cubs

from the Pontiac's window.
No one saw the powerful, frantic mother
spring from the car's rear

rising on her hind legs,
a sudden dark storm cloud.
Swiping at my baby sister's blonde hair.

Screaming we shoved Janice to the floor.
The black paw startled with strings
of gold wheat.

Our mother cursing.
Our father grinding the gears,
"We'll remember this trip" he cackled.

His ventures, his substitutes for guidance.
Always rousing in his four children,
one anxiety or another.

DARK WINGS

Sometimes in one of his Cessna moods,
        my dad would fly over the house
buzzing us with the whirl and whine
        of his twin propellers.
For a moment, were blinded in the bright
        sunlight until we spotted dark wings
outlining his shadow.

Frantically we would wave,
        crossing our arms in human x's,
shouting to the startled neighbors:
        That's our dad! That's our dad!

How small we must have looked to him—
        the maroon matchbox Pontiac
parked in the postage stamp driveway
        dotted with toy children, toy wife,
his toy responsibilities
        growing smaller and paler
as he lifted back
        into the blistering eye
of the sun
        away from us.

SUMMER PIE

In home-sewn matching pink dresses,
we're pressed together
like strawberries in a summer pie.

Behind us, June's long shadows
weave among the elms of Border Park.
Our tones, hushed, delicate.

Primed for a photo, three fresh sisters
propped next to the chrome of the Pontiac's grill.
Its running board dates us: late forties.

Part of its license plate, G290, is peeking out
behind Barbara's skirt, the way our baby sister,
Janice is peeking at the lens.

But we all stand at attention
beneath the car's steel silhouette
waiting for the photographer, our father, to snap

another moment. Obedient Barbara is smiling.
Janice squints in the June sun. We all cringe
from the fire of our father's commands.

But I, already the pouting rebel,
refuse to follow his orders in those hours,
years, decades that followed the forties,

that brutal time
when war was still a wound,
and survival was a small heart, beating.

THE LAST STAR

My mother is like your mother—she is the satiny night.
        Five silver stars spun from her body;
four of them fell to earth. The fifth, the last star, burnt out in the sky.
        That was my brother, Brian Neil, the second son
my father sought, named, but incomplete, who came

                too early that Christmas Eve when the red blinking
of the ambulance
                outshone the crimson lights on the tree.
In the blue cold Alberta night,
                where the case of Coca Cola froze on the back porch,
my mother was rushed to the hospital.
                Later that night, when he told us, your mother lost the baby,
my father's voice was strangely soft, his face dazed
                as a startled buck.

That week he fed us lopsided turkey sandwiches
                and cold mashed potatoes.
Instead of milk, he treated us to fizzy cokes;
                he shared his cashews, the ones he hid in the garage.
        When we picked out the raisins in the Christmas cake,
he ignored it.
                Then he opened the box of Black Magic
chocolates he'd been saving. After five we all felt better.

For the next six nights the menu was repeated until it was
                depleted. While he was at work we ate peanuts for breakfast,
popcorn
                for lunch. We developed stomach aches while our hearts ached.
        But we were fun-centered,
self-centered, and we soon forgot our grief, played
                our new Monopoly around the clock,
not missing the brother, we had never known.

Our mother returned, thinner that white ribbon trimming
                the tree.
She sat by the gas fire, gazing into the blue cone of the flame.
                She smoked, smoked, smoked.

Her haze and her hush filling up the house
            though my asthmatic brother begged her to stop,
while my sisters and I pleaded for her to say our names.
            But she stayed silver cold,
silent as a star.

DESIGNS

Before I was conceived
that late May night
when my father, the flying instructor
was training pilots to rotate
and ready the advance
of their lines of flight
over the silver skies of Saskatchewan,

did my parents talk about creating me,
a third child in their fourth year
of marriage?
Or was I a random genetic drift?
A matter of moonlight?
An iridescent drop
of desire?

No, my father **wanted** a second son.
Another male to model him, to model
airplanes of glue, paper, and popsicle sticks.
He wanted Brian Neil. He got a girl child
who would watch her father and brother
level the wooden wings,
spin the plastic propeller to pitch forward
into a blur of white whirling wind.
Pin up the B52 posters
with their massive fuselages
shaped like sausages.

She would watch behind that gauged
blue-red instrument panel,
the one that navigates
the heart.

HER SUNFLOWER APRON

When Ginny Reuben's kitten, Tickle, got stuck in our giant elm tree, the neighbors flooded our front yard as if free food samples were being offered. The kids jumped, screamed, and cried, trying to coax the frightened creature back down to safe earth.

It was a sunny Saturday morning, so most neighbor men were home. They huddled in tight circles, smoking their Rothmans, surveying the scene. *Get a ladder*, Mister Preshing said, but he didn't move. Just took another drag. *Call the fire department*, Mister Tulloch added, not moving either. The other men nodded but did nothing as the kids waved and wailed.

Suddenly, our front door flew open. And wearing tight yellow shorts, yellow top and her sunflower apron, our mother ran down the stairs, kicked off her sandals, and shimmied up the elm like an agile monkey. She lifted the shaking kitten, set it in her apron pocket and scurried back down just as quickly as she had ascended.

The women cheered and clapped. *Good show, Anne*, our British neighbor stated. My mother handed the kitten to Ginny. She was crying so hard, she couldn't talk. Instead, she hugged my mother as hard as she could. One of the kids chirped, *Mrs. Anderson, you're my hero*.

I turned to the cluster of silent males. No words. No congratulations. Even at eight, I understood their embarrassment. No ladder. No fire department was used. These men had been out-actioned, out-climbed, and out-couraged by a slender, aproned mother of four. They turned, red-faced, slumped and walked out of our yard in their tight, he-man circle.

When I turned to our mother, a small, serene smile had settled on her freckled face.

THE BLUE DIALS

Usually, he gets up in the blue darkness.
Usually it's a single engine, his favorite
silver Cessna 180, that he has polished himself.
Usually, it's a pipeline check or a medical emergency.

My father, the bush pilot, seeking distant stars
of northern Alberta, those cold orbits of Grand Prairie,
Fort Chipewyan, Lac La Biche.

I hear him dressing in the next bedroom.
I know his wardrobe: long sleeved white shirt,
red diamond tie, gold plated cuff links, dark gabardine
trousers, size eleven black wingtips polished like lacquer.

Downstairs he adds his brown leather aviation jacket
and gray felt hat with the tiny amber feather.
His heart anticipates

his fingers on the gray half wheel,
the glide down the darkened runway,
the acceleration, the acceleration
to that turbulent point, that kiss

of land speed, air flow, wing
shape and that deep wind
of his sole propeller

to spin him from the earth
in that shrill thrilled exhilaration of lift.
And my father leaves the planet

with only his love of the air
and the blue dials
on the gray panel to pilot him

as he floats above the Athabasca Tar Sands,
slipping deeper into that black
cosmos, until there is no Earth,
no gravity, no point   that calls him home.

ELEMENTS

With bold diagonal strokes,
Mr. Wakawich, our science teacher
wrote on the blackboard:
C
       A
           R
              B
                  O
                      N.

He tossed the chalk casually into the air,
a flaky stick of pale learning
which identify elements, stabilize isotopes,
calculate specific gravity.

Hand-waving, never incorrect, class genius,
Orest Kewan volunteered: *Carbon.*
A non-metallic chemical element
with the symbol C, atomic number 6,
the most abundant element in the earth's crust...

It was early June, our class was reviewing for finals,
but my eyes were locked on the alpine asters
bursting in purple joy outside the window,
bathed in full magnetic sun.

Oh God! How I wanted to be out there
lounging in my cobalt bikini as my bones
grew colder in the metallic gray chair.
Orest's graveled voice that wouldn't shut up.

The periodic chart is beginning to blur.
And the clock hadn't moved
since I last looked up.
 And I knew I would die
in that 9th grade science classroom
on the hottest recorded summer day
in Alberta.

ZIG-ZAG

My mother watched the kitchen clock
      as if her life was ticking down:
6:03, 6:17, 6:31. Our hunger clanging like copper
      wind chimes on the back
porch: 6:47, 6:52, 7:03, waiting, waiting
      for our father, the pilot to return.
While we picked at the roast, sneaked cucumber slices,
      dipped our rude fingers
into the gravy, I could taste my mother's disappointment.
      Finally, we hurried through lukewarm potatoes, wilted salad,
sinewy roast, anxious to get back to our fortune
      on *Pacific Avenue*, solve the vital secret
in *The Scarlet Slipper Mystery*,
      or play with our wacky budgie, Binky
who pecked out neat pink triangles of Monopoly fives.
      It could have been cozy after-dinner scene—
our grandfather's honey tobacco pipe
      mingling in the air of the noisy November night,
but our father was missing;
      he was always missing out
on our lives.

Once when he was home, he fed Binki rum and coke
      in a plastic tangerine cup. She sipped,
sipped, sipped
      then stepped rolled side-to-side,
zigzagged, in her drunken dance, and my father howled, clapped
      in rhythm to whirs of her citrus-colored feathers.
She skidded down the table,
      landed in the butter,
sank into its soft yellowness.
      Her bright red eyes blazing in panic
My sisters and I screamed.
      Our father snorted with laughter
as Binki's small slick feathers quivered
      when she tried to unfold them,

tried to lift, tried her damnedest
        to ascend
out of grease
        and chaos.

JOHNNY TWO FEATHERS

Moccasin summer.
Smoky hide evenings.
Another red beaded sunset
when Johnny Two Feathers
lent me his buckskin jacket.
Fringes soft, comforting
on my sunburnt legs.

He led me away from the bonfire,
dancers, beer cans crashing.
Led me down to the river birches,
breathing, breathing
in their slender darkness.

His long fingers whispered legends.
His tongue was an arrow darting
in and out of the O's of my mouth,
ears, my eyes.
But his eyes began a blackness
I could not touch.

Johnny Two Feathers,
part Cree, part rage
of a white fathered memory.
Moonlight and river.
Skin rippling into skin
we forgot the empty fridges,
gasless cars, no running water,
broken windows, broken children,
silver fish and cockroaches
landlording the walls.
All August we tried to forget
that sour smell of hopelessness.

DAUGHTER CELL

When the cop stops me doing 50
in a 15 zone of the Foothills Hospital,
glances at my white ensemble, asks if I'm a nurse,
I almost lie my way out
but truth is a tight white stocking
and the words, wrapped around my tongue,
are adhesive, a bandage, trying to cover
my father's frail body seven floors above
hobbling through the cancer ward.
I carry his antiseptic scent into this late May air.

I cannot lie for truth is a stain
oozing blood, bile, vomit and shit,
forming scabs, lesions, tumors, puke, all
the sick nouns of the big C.
And more, because there is always,
always more: Tests, pills, radiation, chemo.
Chemo, radiation, pills, tests.

It takes more
than one person to tell the truth,
Faulkner said. The truth can blind you.
Or maim you. Or cancer you.
Because truth is a serum
of cells spreading far from its origin,
the daughter cell. They carry no life, no purpose
and these cells divide geometrically
in the fucking binomial of 2, 4, 8, 16, 32, 64, 128…
Hungry, these crabs, these cancer claws,
haul through the host until they've eaten
all that the body can feed them
until bones, until stones.

This is the summer of my new vocabulary:
carcinomas, sarcomas, lymphatic, metastasize.
This cop cannot grasp that I cannot sense speed
when there are no limits to pain
and my brain is blurry.

Inside my own membranes, the cells of my son
are lining up like kids at kindergarten.
And he's behind the girl with the long curly ponytail
swishing the way my platinum, young-as-a-swing hair
would swish and fall, fall like my father's hair falling.
I can't stop it. I can't stop being a daughter,
a cell carrying another cell and I've turned into this
muted street where a cop leans into his ticket pad.
And a yellow sign warns what I've supposed all spring: *NO OUTLET.*

OBSERVING THE BUZZARDS

They chose Carolina's Kitty Hawk's shore
because the soft sand would ease
the impact of a crash landing,
because the consistent coasting winds were forceful
could keep a gliding plane aloft
for three seconds,
   twelve seconds,
     seventeen,
       and then, and then—a minute!
    December 17, 1903.
Damned if they ain't flewn! A spectator on the beach shouted.

They got there by bicycle, link-by-link.
Kite-by-kite, a thousand glider kites.
They read. They studied. They wrote
to the renown white-bearded scientist
at the Smithsonian, but he had nose-
dived into the Potomac with his double tandem
winged craft and his $50,000 Army grant.

Self-taught bicycle builders but with engineers' handles,
they concluded that Langley's lift ratios were wholly wrong.
So, Wilbur began observing the buzzards over Dayton.
He noticed when the wind knocked them askew,
they dropped their sweeping wings down, down
to recover their balance.
It was the air behind the wings
like a fresh breath that gives lift to the body.
Persistent as rain, the young brothers re-focused,
redesigned. They curved the wings, built a wind tunnel,
practiced their "wing warping" with strings.
Turned one wing up, the other down.
They created balance and roll. They created controlled
flight.

They added a rudder, a motor, a propeller
connected to the engine with bicycle chains.
They brainstormed. They tested. They tossed

a coin to see which brother would go first,
who would feel his frame lifted
like Icarus with his home-made feathery wings.
Orville won. We all won.

POETIC DUST

A poem should always have a bird in it. Mary Oliver

A poem should always have a bird in it.
Even a small one. Say a pint-size bee
hummingbird, the smallest bird in the world.
So tiny it's mistaken for an insect.

It's like a bonsai bird, reduced to its
miniaturized self of onyx-black beak
and iridescent teal coat that shimmers like a jewel.

Small, but splendid, this bird can fly straight up.
Straight down. Straight backwards. And like a
F-18 Fighter jet, even upside down.

Slight, but plump with upper plumage and busy wings
that beat 80 times per second. A busier bill and protractile
tongue, it visits a thousand nectar-dripping blossoms daily

to pollinate the flora of Cuba's Zapata Swamp,
coastal forests and mountain valleys while it
spreads flowery pollen and poetic dust.

Because every bird should always have a poem in it.

ACE OF DIAMONDS

Luck is where you find it, my father,
the bush pilot used to say.
He arm-wrestled another pilot
for my mother's engagement ring.

Hung a rabbit's foot
on the rear-view mirror
of the '51 Chieftain

where it swung like a promise.
Played poker on Thursdays.
Friday nights, BINGO.

Once he tied for a $4,000 prize.
His consolation—32 pieces of *Mel Mac*
that he tried to break, hammer-smash,

crush beneath the Pontiac's front wheels.
Indestructible turquoise cups,
lemon plates, tangerine platter
that tinted our table each morning.

He looked for luck everywhere.
Among black columned numbers
of the racing form.
Between high silver wings of his Cessna.
Deep inside his secretary's cleavage.

And when cancer trumped him
in October, he refused to believe
that his luck had run out.
Kept booking flights.

Ordered summer roses
from his Burpee catalogue.
*Ace of Diamonds: A double red bloom
with few thorns.
Good at resisting diseases*

TWO PHONE CALLS

Bad news arrives over black cables
from Boston. From Calgary.
Two friends, both fifty, both dead.
Cancer. Cardiac arrest.

I peel potatoes, carrots, onions
as if the scraping damp chore
will sponge my sadness.
My tears outrun the onions' tears.

Outside the pin oak is leafing.
The air mists with sap and spring
and shades of arbors and emeralds
animated with lemon-lime light.
The earth pungent with wet woods.

In the pan, soft cuttings of meat
surrender their redness.
Juices drain to brown.
The stew slowly simmers.

Textures float sinewy
as threaded veins.
Vegetables distinguish themselves—
organic pigmentations
like leaves in autumn
when one season lies down
for another.

RUNWAY LIGHTS

As I lift your wrinkled daisies,
out of the depression-green vase,

they scatter like soft snowflakes.
White bodies tumbling into the air.

I think of your noon plane hovering
in the frost over Heathrow.

It's been a winter of blue farewells,
a cobalt season of airports:

New Delhi   Vancouver   Pittsburgh
Landings   and   takeoffs

executed in high velocity, or low
visibility. Always in elevated emotion.

The blue runway lights resemble azure lines
of travelers who dare to discover.

Emigrants, who dare to cross over.
Propelled by jet, fueled with desire,

passengers arrive faster than the sounds
of their own hollow voices

which echo inside a detached terminal
where courtesy is a white telephone.

And anxiety paces
like a jet black wing.

SUITS

My father always wore a suit and tie in flight.
Was it because he still longed for that striking blue
RCAF uniform he swaggeringly wore during the war?

Or did he want to be like Orville Wright
who constantly dressed up for his landings?
Even the crash landings.

And how many crashes did my father endure
giving flying lessons, critical medical flights,
pipeline cruising?

Each time his spine tattered,
the chiropractor would put it back,
disk-by-disk.

My mother always believed
his ending would come in a wreck.
His Cessna plummeted belly-up.
She'd pace in his lateness.
Gasp when a phone call clattered
in the dead of night.
Start to shiver with a radio report
of a downed pilot.

But it was the soar
of white-winged cells
that would claim him.

First in the throat,
then they descended into the liver.
Finally gliding into his kidneys
with their deadly, vibrating sounds:
Whir. Quiver. Tremble.

With each parachute of pain, his flesh fell.
His cheek bones protruded like propellers.

And when they folded him into his old uniform,
it slipped around him, a dark blue shroud,
floating above cloudy, white silk.

DEAR MISS MANNERS

Thank you for your prompt note.
Now I know where I should seat the ex-
husband of my former mother-in-law's stepson
who's separated from our third cousin
from my father's fifth marriage.
Etiquette is tricky
and getting stickier than Velcro.

For instance, what **does** a civil woman say
to her shaking lover
who gets a severe leg cramp
just at that sweet penetrating moment?
Shake it honey! Shake it!
Walk it off!
Try some ice on it!

Appropriateness is so fucking hard.

I've been told by a genteel lady
that the Junior League
doesn't believe in group sex
because they are too many thank you cards
to send.

Manners, my mother used to lecture—
are what separate us from the apes.
Don't eat out of the bag like a baboon,
she'd chew out Larry with his elbow
deep in Old Dutch potato chips.
She caught Barbara and me
in our sunflower seed spitting contest.
You're not chimpanzees!

But we were teenagers,
that time when those primate lines
of gestured civility
and orangutan comportment

are drawn in charcoal.
Easily smudged.
Easily erased.

SUNDERANCE

The barber flaps the cutting sheet across my son's chest.
Woven into the waiting chairs are pale satin weaves.
I finger them curiously.
Parachute cords from World War II,
the barber explains between wads of tobacco
and pumps of the pedal
as my young son elevates
high, high, higher into the air.

Halfway around the room he revolves
to spy on himself in the glass.
The rusty October sunlight glazes
the scissors' silver teeth.
A steel blade disappears inside
my son's soft chestnut hair.
Clip.
Clip.
Clip.
His swirls of dark hair drop
into the air like parachutes…

And I think of the smoking fields of Hanover,
my uncle, Willard, nineteen, harnessed in the gunner's seat,
his RCAF wings pinned like a moth's
beneath the flaming circle of steel,
RAT-TA-TA-TAT of the anti-aircraft fire,
flames, charred flesh, cries darker than smoke,
somber scream of sirens.
The wingless plane marries the German soil.

Three decades later in the Allied Cemetery,
my mother kneels at her brother's grave.
She sobs uncontrollably, not with grief but rage,
never forgiving "the dirty Krauts"

never cutting loose
the white silky cords of her loss.

WHAT WE DO FOR OUR CHILDREN

The Australian shepherd, the cocker spaniel,
both squirm when I load them into the Passport.
Both belong to my daughter.
It's been a month of canine care.
While she breezes the beaches and bars of LA,
I'm plucking fleas, picking up dog shit.

What we do for our children!
We do what our parents did. Or didn't.
How many strays did I drag home?
One eyed tabby, neglected retriever,
erratic boyfriend. My parents shrieked
but relented. *Just for one night*
in that halfway house on 91st street,
where kids, relations, and drifters
revolved like spent spokes.

Now, as wives, what we do for our spouses!
We listen and listen until our ears fold into lips.
Some speak. Some swear. Some stay silent
as yellowed photos of old lovers.
And what we did for them
is what we wanted,
still want for ourselves-
the sweet worship of our bodies' wounds.

SLIPPING

When I slipped out of my gold sandals,
  and slid them casually onto the rug,
    I didn't plan for them to be perfectly placed
      in opposite directions
        before I slipped into bed
          where my husband was slipping into something
          comfortable, a silky dream,

but there they were,
  one sandal facing east,
    its right-footed twin looking westward.
      It just happened,
        my neighbor said,
          when he told me about our other neighbor
          who slipped off the east ramp of I-75

and sailed west though the open window,
  without a seatbelt, without a word.
    It just happened
      the way his widow wrapped her grief
        around stringed cardboard boxes
          when we offered our clumsy condolences,

the compass of her heart spinning
  as her husband slipped away from her
    like a slipper,
      a secret,
      a life.

So, she turns north,
  returning to Ohio, the buckeye state,
    home to seven Presidents,
    and the Wright Brothers

      who learned to slip into the air,
      and gave us all a lift
      when they showed us
      how to spin bicycles
      into wings.

THE FIRST BOY I KISSED

The first boy I kissed, Jerry Rubin,
lived next door.
Does that still count?

He was Protestant.
I was Catholic.
We were a hundred sacraments apart.

The kiss was quick
and ordinary,
dry as yesterday.

I didn't even have time
to close my eyes like the movie star
girls in the Saturday movies.

Later when I confessed
to my Saint Joseph's classmates,
there was an audible gasp.

They didn't say, you kissed a boy.
They hissed in unison:
You kissed a PROTESANT!

As if I had kissed
a blind goat
with leprosy.

Jerry grew up and moved away,
I grew weary of Catholic Catechism.
Doctrine. Constrictions.

Maybe that's why I married a Hindu.
And the first time I kissed Ravi
it was royal and long and wet
and I thought...
Hare Krishna!
Hare Ram!

BAGELS

They're hiring at the Bagel Shop.
Maybe I should apply?
Trade my lesson plan/grade book
for that chic black cap and apron?
Hey, I'm experienced with the blackboard.
I could chalk those specials with quick neat letters:

HOT SHOT TURKEY

I'd bring my other teaching skills.
I'd coach and convince the customers
not to choose a cup of soup,
but a brimming bowl of chicken noodle
or a garden salad with fresh-
from-the-earth vegetables.
Notice the crunch of the grated carrots,
pungency of the plump tomatoes,
those fine thin diced onions.

And when I spread that dreamy creamy dairy cheese
across the face of a warm bagel, it would be lovingly
the way I once spread the word of imagery.
Of course, there's always the danger I'd overdo
the alliteration of those old-fashioned bagels.
I might push pumpkin cream cheese on a pumpernickel
or smoked salmon on sesame.
Honey walnut on a honey grain might be too obvious.
I'd go for antonyms: wild berry on a tame plain one.
Jalapeno on a chocolate chip.

I'd never quit. I'd lecture
on the history of Leonardo da Veggie.
Help clients design their own bagel sandwiches.
Give bonus points of sprouts, tomatoes, and onions.

But like all ordained teachers, I'd test them:
Name the 15 bagel flavors. Identify six kinds of cream cheese.
But then I'm back to where I started. I've come full bagel.

Do all jobs take on the profession
of what we desire?
I'm a teacher. Every workplace is a school.
And at this shop, the bagels are like my students.
They don't come any fresher.

TAMPA LIGHTS

December dusk.
These clouds are coral streaks
against an azure sky.
                    As we coast down the tarmac,
                    scarlet lights, royal blue lights
                    brighten the gray runway.
Then our wheels start to whizz
like buzzard wings.
as thrust rides on the plane's back
and pushes it forward
                    into the amethyst twilight.
                    Twilight—the word hangs in the air,
                    lingers like port tingling the tongue.

Suddenly speed shakes
and vibrates the aircraft
until the heart's thrill of lift
and we are airborne
quickly as a peregrine falcon.

                    Below us, the lights of Tampa sparkle
                    like a thousand upside-down stars.
                    Tampa, home of traders, pirates,
                    cigars and tropical storms.

Tampa, meaning *sticks of fire*,
named accurately by the Calusa.
Tampa, now the lightning capital
of North America.

                    But tonight, Tampa slides away from us
                    as we advance into the clouds.
                    As we find our way
                    floating among the dark
                    vapors of altitudes, directions,
                    dreams.

GAIL GHAI is a poet, Pushcart Prize nominee, recipient of a Henry C. Frick scholarship for creative teaching, frequent presenter for the Florida Writers Association and author of three poetry chapbooks. Her poems have appeared in *Poet Lore, The Delhi-London Quarterly, Descant* and *Shot Glass Journal.* She is a moderator of the Ringling Poets in Sarasota, FL.

www.ingramcontent.com/pod-product-compliance
Lightning Source LLC
Chambersburg PA
CBHW020223090426
42734CB00008B/1191